CRAZY

JUST

MIGHT

WORK.

THIS IS FOR THE DREAMERS, THE
GETTERS. THIS IS FOR THE INN
THE RISK TAKERS, THE CHANGE
THE SHAKERS, THE DISRUPTERS
FOR THE ARTISTS, THE CREATIVE

THIS IS

BECAUSE YOU HAVE SOMETHING
WONDER OF THIS WONDERFUL WOR
BEAUTIFUL, UNBELIEVABLE IDEAS.
AND THEY ARE JUST GETTING S

DOERS, THE BELIEVERS, THE GO-
VATORS, THE ENTREPRENEURS,
AKERS. THIS IS FOR THE MOVERS,
THE THOUGHT LEADERS. THIS IS
THE LOVERS, THE ADVENTURERS.
FOR YOU...
MAGICAL TO CONTRIBUTE TO THE
. SO WELCOME YOUR WILD, CRAZY,
EY ARE HERE FOR A REASON
RTED.

THOUSANDS OF YEARS AGO, MANY BELIEVED THE EARTH WAS FLAT.

FIVE HUNDRED YEARS AGO, WE WERE SURE THE SUN WAS THE CENTER OF THE UNIVERSE.

IMAGINE WHAT WE WILL LEARN TOMORROW THAT WILL DISPROVE WHAT WE BELIEVE TODAY.

BE COURAGEOUS IN YOUR CURIOSITY.

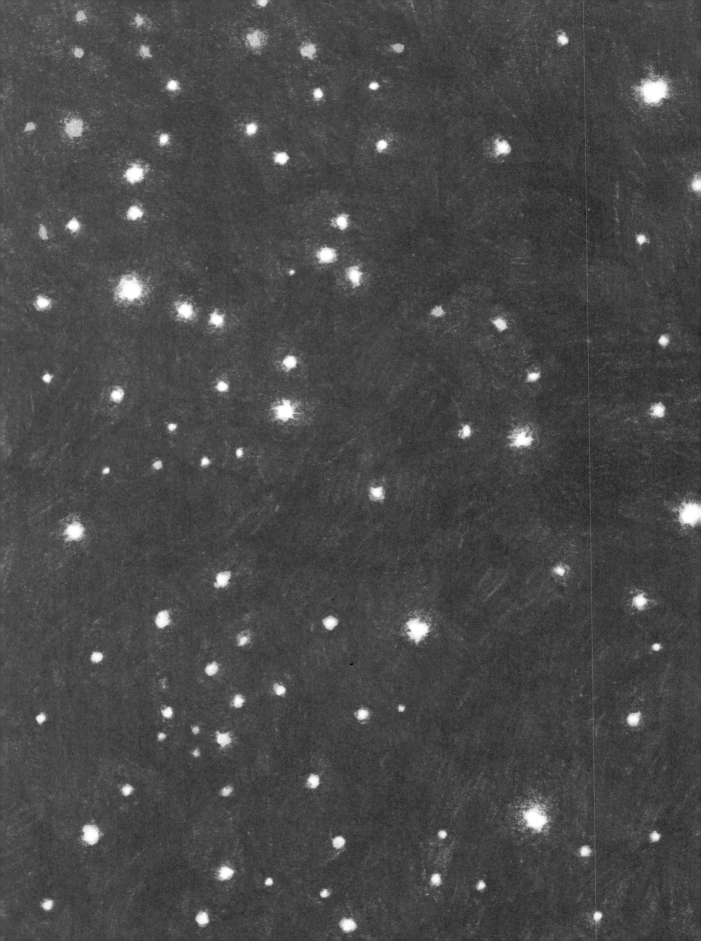

Thoughts are like burning stars, and ideas, they flood, they stretch the universe.

CRISS JAMI

WHERE

Where do you find inspiration?

DOES

In a book? Hidden in a song lyric? Whispered amongst the trees?

INSPIRATION

In a crowded coffee shop? In total silence? Dancing in the waves?

FIND

With the wind in your face? With sweat dripping off your chin?

YOU?

CREATIVELY, I HAVE THE MOST ENERGY WHEN:

WE NEED TO MAKE THE WORLD SAFE FOR CREATIVITY AND INTUITION, FOR IT'S CREATIVITY AND INTUITION THAT WILL MAKE THE WORLD SAFE FOR US.

Edgar Mitchell

NEVER STOP
CREATING

WHAT ARE YOU WORRIED ABOUT?

List as many things as you can:

....

....

....

....

....

....

....

....

....

....

....

....

....

WHERE ARE THE BIG OPPORTUNITIES IF NOT HIDDEN INSIDE OUR BIGGEST PROBLEMS?

WHAT AND WHO DO YOU APPRECIATE OR ADMIRE?

List as many things and people as you can:

WHAT OR WHO
CAN YOU MODEL
TO INSPIRE YOU?

IF YOU NOTICE ANYTHING, IT LEADS YOU TO NOTICE MORE AND MORE.

Mary Oliver

what if...

what if...

what if...

PAY CLOSE ATTENTION TO THE THING
THAT COMES AFTER THE WORDS, "WHAT IF..."

what if...

what if...

what if...

TELL
STORIES

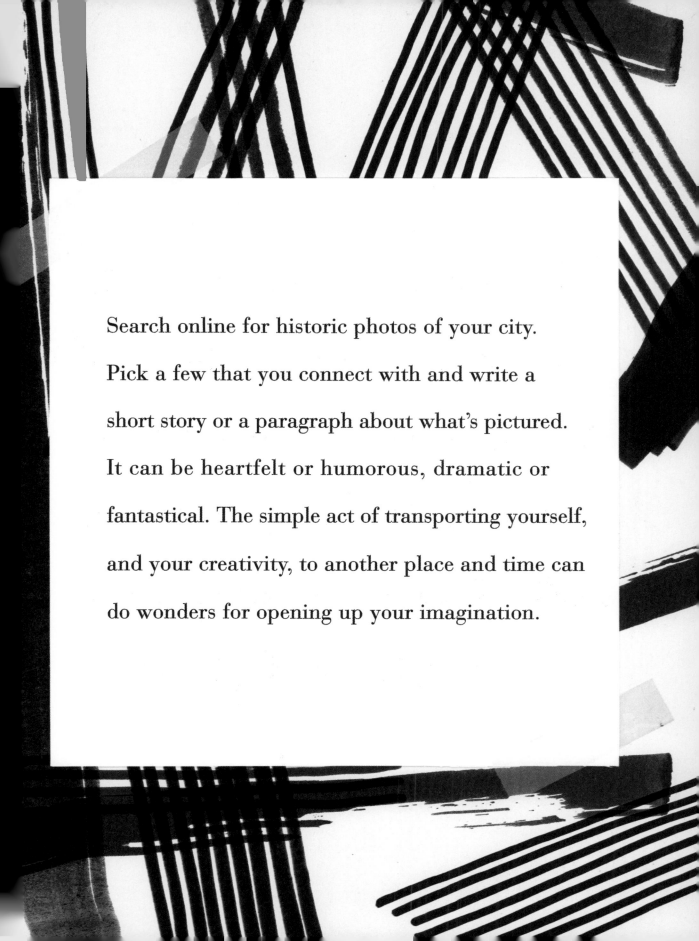

Search online for historic photos of your city. Pick a few that you connect with and write a short story or a paragraph about what's pictured. It can be heartfelt or humorous, dramatic or fantastical. The simple act of transporting yourself, and your creativity, to another place and time can do wonders for opening up your imagination.

We are called upon to become creators, to make the world new and in that sense to bring something into being which was not there before.

JOHN ELOF BOODIN

Be a st
THE OR

anger to
DINARY.

By creating a space for daydreaming and encouraging contemplation, you can spur creativity. In a world where we are always connected, it is easy for our brains to be satiated and satisfied. This can stunt your curiosity and your ability to create and generate new ideas. It's important to leave room for pondering. Completely unplug for a while, let your mind wander... and follow where it leads.

THERE IS A VOICE THAT DOESN'T

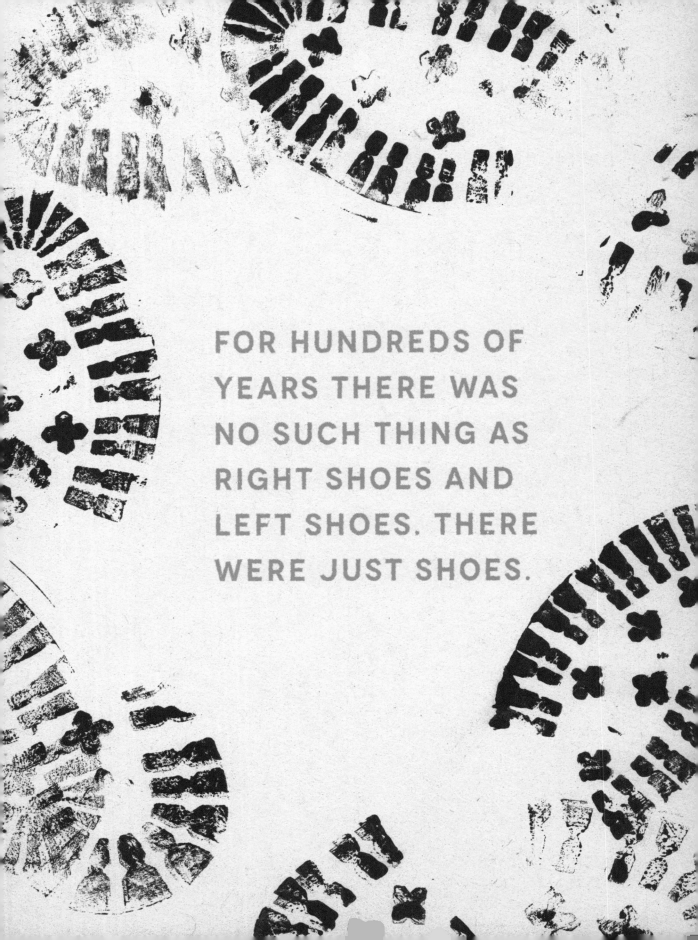

FOR HUNDREDS OF
YEARS THERE WAS
NO SUCH THING AS
RIGHT SHOES AND
LEFT SHOES. THERE
WERE JUST SHOES.

THE MIND, ONCE STRETCHED BY A NEW IDEA, NEVER RETURNS TO ITS ORIGINAL DIMENSIONS.

Ralph Waldo Emerson

PROVE TO
YOURSELF
THAT YOU
CAN DO
SOMETHING
YOU THOUGHT
YOU COULDN'T.

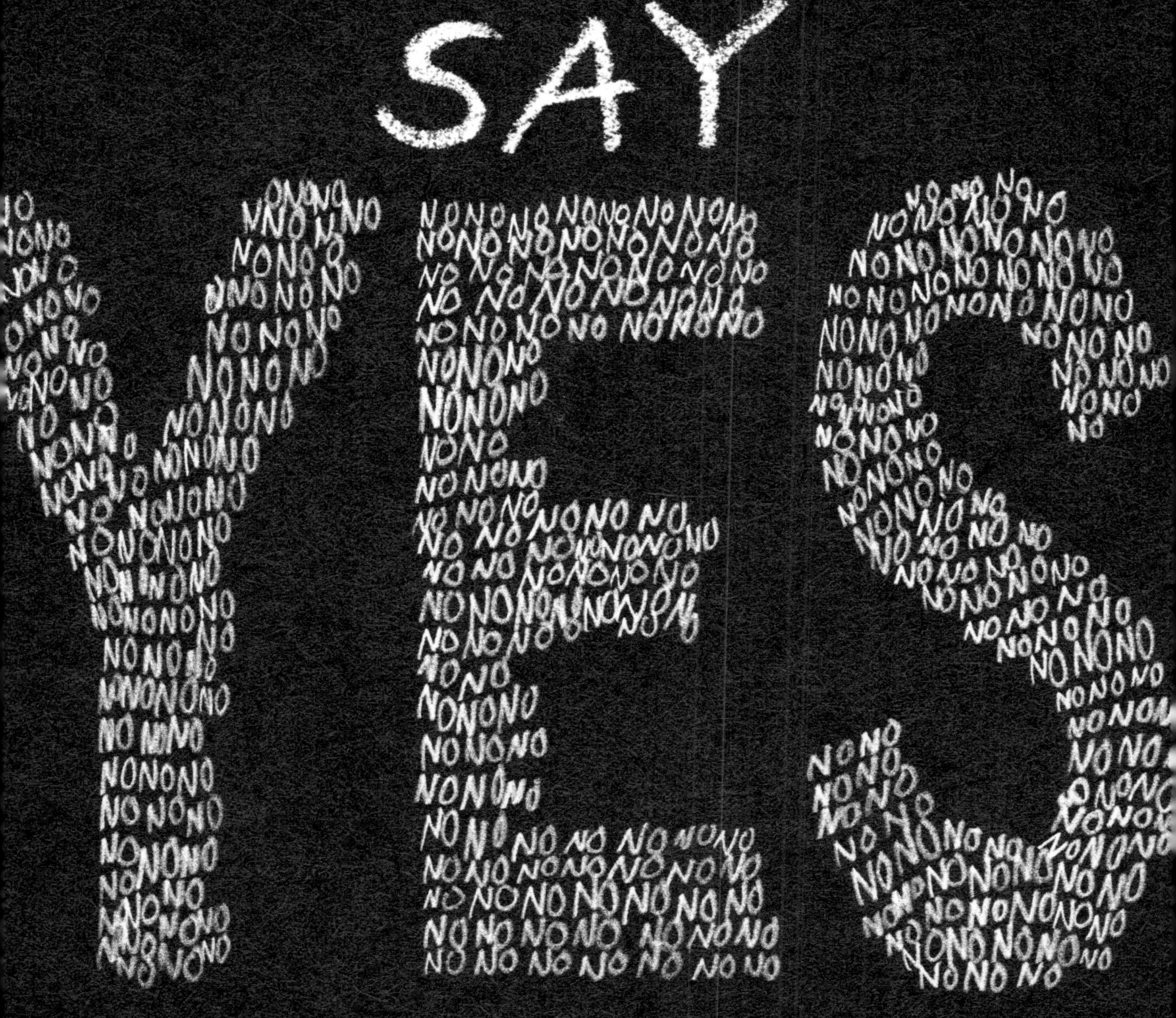
SAY
YES

WHAT IS FAILURE?

IS FAILURE REALLY FAILURE OR COULD IT BE A STEP TO SOMETHING ELSE? MANY OF THE PEOPLE, PRODUCTS, AND IDEAS WE ADMIRE TODAY FAILED PAINFULLY ON THEIR WAY TO EVENTUAL SUCCESS.

Thomas Edison's teachers considered him "too stupid to learn anything" as a youth. He was fired from two jobs as an adult for lack of productivity. He went on to create multiple inventions, such as the lightbulb and phonograph, which have profoundly shaped our world.

Mary Leakey was expelled from every secondary school she attended after continually failing exams and causing an explosion in a chemistry lab. She went on to uncover evidence that gave us groundbreaking insights into human origins and is considered one of the most important paleoanthropologists of our time.

Walt Disney was fired from his job at *The Kansas City Star* because he "lacked imagination." He then founded an animation studio called Laugh-O-Gram Studio, which went bankrupt. But he went on to create Mickey Mouse and Minnie Mouse and the global Disney entertainment empire.

Oprah Winfrey was fired as a coanchor on Baltimore's WJZ-TV after seven months because she was told she was too invested in the stories she was covering. She went on to become a media mogul and create one of the most successful daytime television shows in history.

Jack Ma failed at both preschool and secondary school, was turned down by Harvard 10 times, and had his application rejected by more than 30 different companies for jobs ranging from fast food work to entry level police positions. He went on to earn billions as cofounder of the e-commerce site Alibaba.

Albert Einstein was a poor student who didn't speak until age 4 or read until age 7. He was considered "slow" by family and teachers and was even expelled from school. He went on to win the Nobel Prize and change our understanding of physics forever.

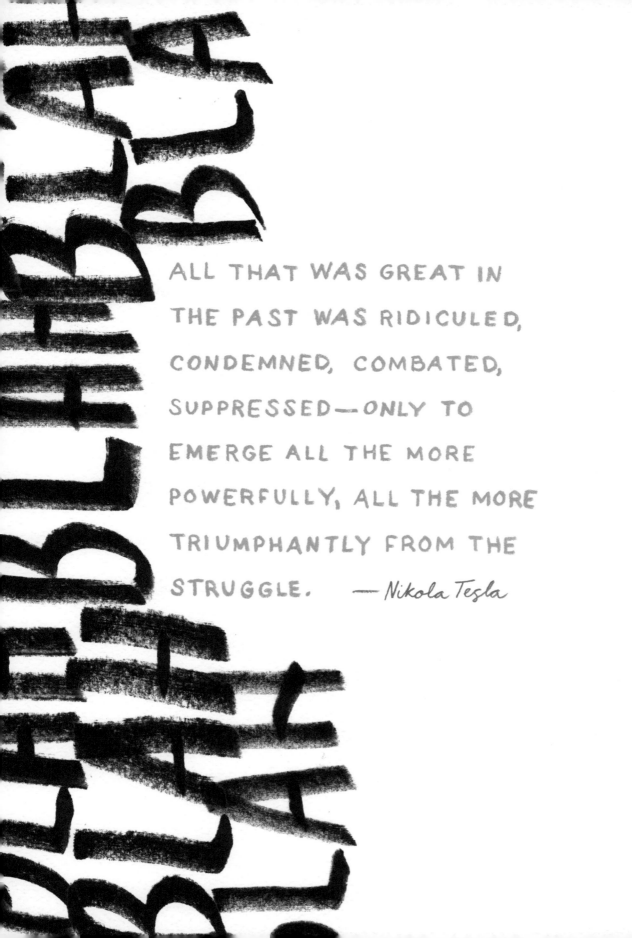

ALL THAT WAS GREAT IN THE PAST WAS RIDICULED, CONDEMNED, COMBATED, SUPPRESSED—ONLY TO EMERGE ALL THE MORE POWERFULLY, ALL THE MORE TRIUMPHANTLY FROM THE STRUGGLE. — *Nikola Tesla*

IF YOU ABSOLUTELY KNEW YOUR IDEA COULD NOT FAIL,

BE BRAVE ENOUGH TO BE
BAD AT ~~SOMTHING~~ NEW.
SOMETHING

IT'S VERY HARD TO HAVE
IDEAS. IT'S VERY HARD TO
PUT YOURSELF OUT THERE.
IT'S VERY HARD TO BE
VULNERABLE, BUT THOSE
PEOPLE THAT DO THAT ARE
THE DREAMERS, AND THE
THINKERS, AND THE CREATORS.
AND THEY ARE THE MAGIC
PEOPLE OF THE WORLD.

Amy Poehler

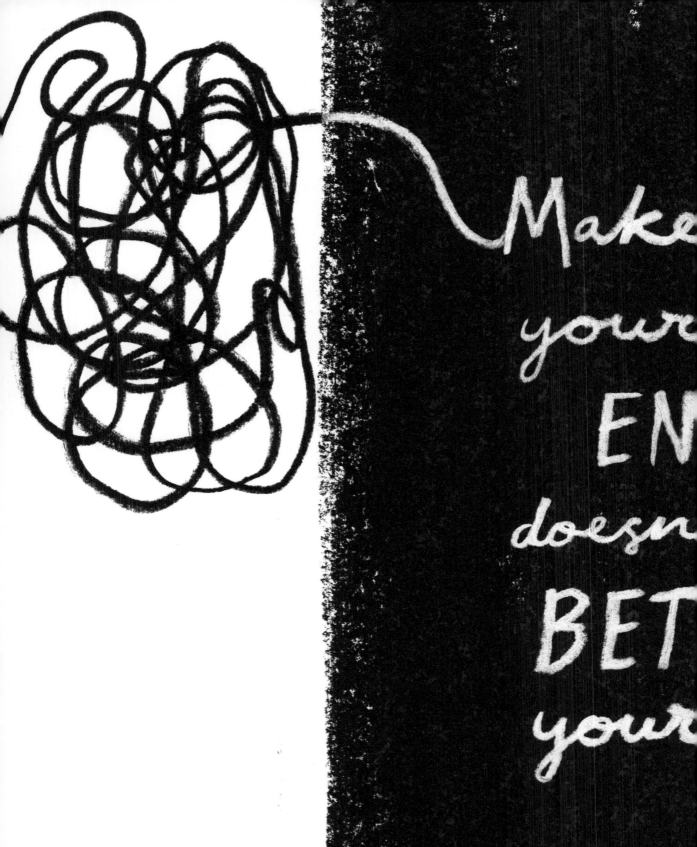

Make
your
EN
doesn
BET
your

sure

worst

EMY

t live

WEEN

ears.

PRACTICE RANDOM ACTS OF CREATIVITY

Make a piece of art that is inspiring or encouraging. It could be a poem, a painting, a sculpture, or a handwritten note. Leave it anonymously in a public place, like a park or library. Just make sure it is somewhere it can be found. When you are creating it, think about the person who may happen upon it. What is their life like? How is their day going? What will this unexpected gift mean to them, discovering it in this unexpected way? This generous and selfless act of creativity will open up both the heart and the head, and will help you feel connected to those around you.

...STEP FORWARD INTO GROWTH OR STEP BACK INTO SAFETY.

ABRAHAM MASLOW

...WHAT MAKES YOU DIFFERENT OR WEIRD... IS PART OF HUMAN NATURE. IT CAN ONLY BE UNTAUGHT.

AI WEIWEI

OVERRATED

CREATIVITY TAKES COURAGE.

HENRI MATISSE

THAT IS YOUR STRENGTH.

MERYL STREEP

DEFINITIONS BELONG TO THE DEFINERS, NOT THE DEFINED.

TONI MORRISON

NORMAL IS

CREATIVITY

BE THE ANTIDOTE FOR ALL THE UNORIGINAL THINKING THAT'S GOING ON AROUND YOU.

DELORES RODRIGUEZ

If you're(e) not
(tr) perpared to be
(w)rong, you'll
never come up
with anything
~~origional~~ (x)
ORIGINAL

SIR KEN ROBINSON

SOMETIMES, MANY TIMES,

WRONG

HELPS US FIND

RIGHT.

THE GOOD, AND THE NOT
SO GOOD, BOTH TEACH.

OPEN YOUR MIND, YOUR EYES, AND YOUR HEART TO NEW WAYS OF THINKING AND FEELING.

XMI ITHSNG PU

IMX NISGTH UP

XIM SGNIHT PU

MIX THINGS UP

XMI HTISNG PU

IMX GIHNTS UP

XIM SGNIHT PU

EAT YOUR MEALS, BRUSH YOUR TEETH, SIGN YOUR NAME WITH YOUR NON-DOMINANT HAND. RESEARCH SHOWS THESE LITTLE CHALLENGES CAN LEAD TO EXPANSION IN THE CORTEX THAT CONTROLS AND PROCESSES TACTILE INFORMATION.

SOMEWHERE, HIDDEN, IS A BETTER WAY OF DOING THINGS.

Harry Bertoia

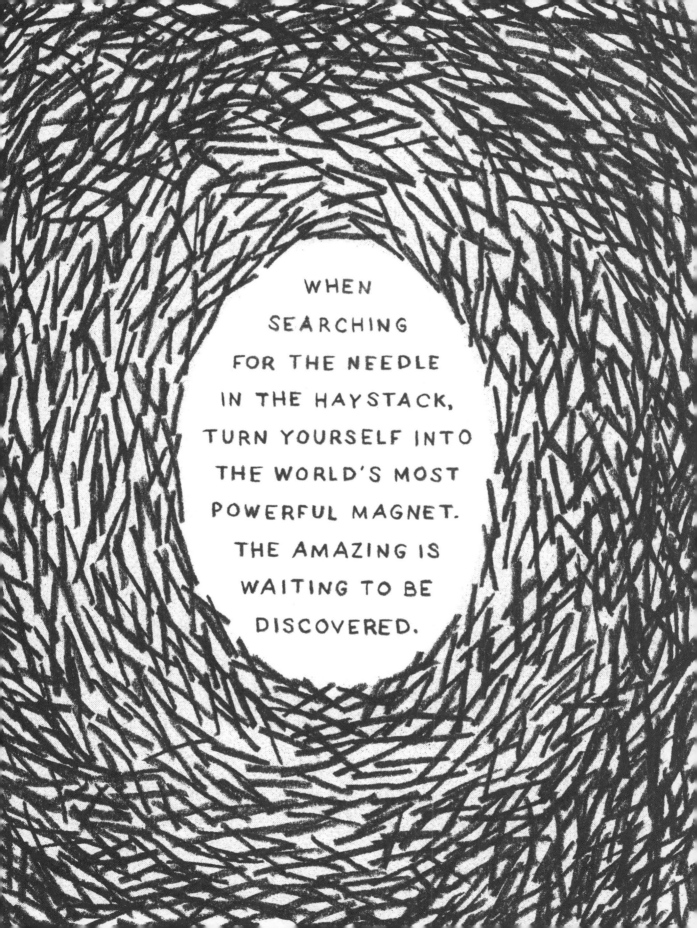

WHEN
SEARCHING
FOR THE NEEDLE
IN THE HAYSTACK,
TURN YOURSELF INTO
THE WORLD'S MOST
POWERFUL MAGNET.
THE AMAZING IS
WAITING TO BE
DISCOVERED.

THE SECRET TO CHANGE IS
TO FOCUS ALL OF YOUR ENERGY,
NOT ON FIGHTING THE OLD,

BUT ON BUILDING THE NEW.

Dan Millman

WHERE DO YOU DRAW THE LINE BETWEEN *possible* AND IMPOSSIBLE?

STAY

FOCUSED

Multitasking is a misnomer.

If you really want to channel

your creative power, you will

achieve more if you allow your

focus to be uninterrupted

for at least 15 minutes at a time.

When you're learning to play a new song, give it your full attention and energy. Then walk away

and give the music time to reach your fingertips.

ELYSA FENENBOCK

INHABIT
YOUR
MOMENTS.

INHABIT YOUR MOMENTS.

Name 7 works of art (literature, visual ar

_____

_____

_____

_____

_____

_____

WHAT DO YOUR SELECTIONS HAVE IN COMMON
WHAT INTERESTS YOU CAN INFOR

...rchitecture) that mean something to you.

_____

_____

_____

_____

_____

_____

DO YOU SEE ANY SIMILARITIES OR PATTERNS?

AND INSPIRE WHAT YOU CREATE.

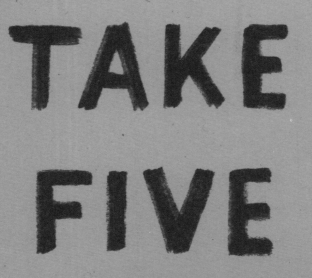

While it's important to focus and concentrate, it is just as important to give your brain a break. Try this: Take a break from whatever you are doing for at least five minutes to reset your brain. Do this five times throughout the day. Stilling your mind breaks its rhythm and causes it to refresh. Which means it can return to tasks with increased perspective and creativity, sort of like "interval training" for your brain.

Through the mere act of creating something—anything—you might inadvertently produce work that is magnificent, eternal, or important...

ELIZABETH GILBERT

SOME IDEAS SPARK.

SOME IDEAS FLOW.

AND SOME IDEAS

YOU NEED TO

HAMMER AND FORGE

INTO BEING.

REALITY CAN BE BEATEN WITH ENOUGH IMAGINATION.

MARK TWAIN

Light is as powerful as a drug, and if you use it right you can enhance your energy and focus. Exposure to blue light, the same light that comes from the sun, increases brain activity and alertness more than drinking a cup of coffee. It also speeds up reaction time and impacts circadian rhythm, the internal clock that controls your sleep schedule. So go outside, and take a 10-minute walk to increase alertness and recharge.

When a flower doesn't bloom, you fix the environment in which it grows, not the flower.

ALEXANDER DEN HEIJER

DARE TO BELIEVE, THE WHISPERS IN YOUR EARS, THAT YOU MIGHT BE SPECIAL, THAT YOU MIGHT BE MEANINGFUL, THAT ONE DAY YOU MIGHT CHANGE THE WORLD.

ATTICUS

BREATHE
DEEP

Lack of inspiration can come from being too much in your head (worrying about what others think) and not enough in your heart (feeling connected). Try this meditative breathing exercise to clear out the fog and get you centered: Sit in a comfortable position. Bring your palms together (this helps to bring the left and right hemispheres of your brain back in balance). Inhale to a count of four through the nose. Exhale to a count of four through the nose. Continue doing this for three minutes. To end, inhale to fully expand your lungs and exhale.

HOW WILL YOU
BEAUTIFUL TO

GIVE SOMETHING THE WORLD?

THE IDEA IS NOT TO LIVE FOREVER, IT IS TO CREATE SOMETHING THAT WILL.

Andy Warhol

YOU ARE ONLY
ONE IDEA AWAY
FROM CHANGING
everything.

To Dan Zadra,

A creative genius and the one whose idea started it all.

WITH SPECIAL THANKS TO THE ENTIRE COMPENDIUM FAMILY.

Credits:
Written by: Kobi Yamada
Edited by: Amelia Riedler
Designed by: Jessica Phoenix

Library of Congress Control Number: 2018955811
ISBN: 978-1-946873-59-0

1st printing. Printed in China with soy inks.

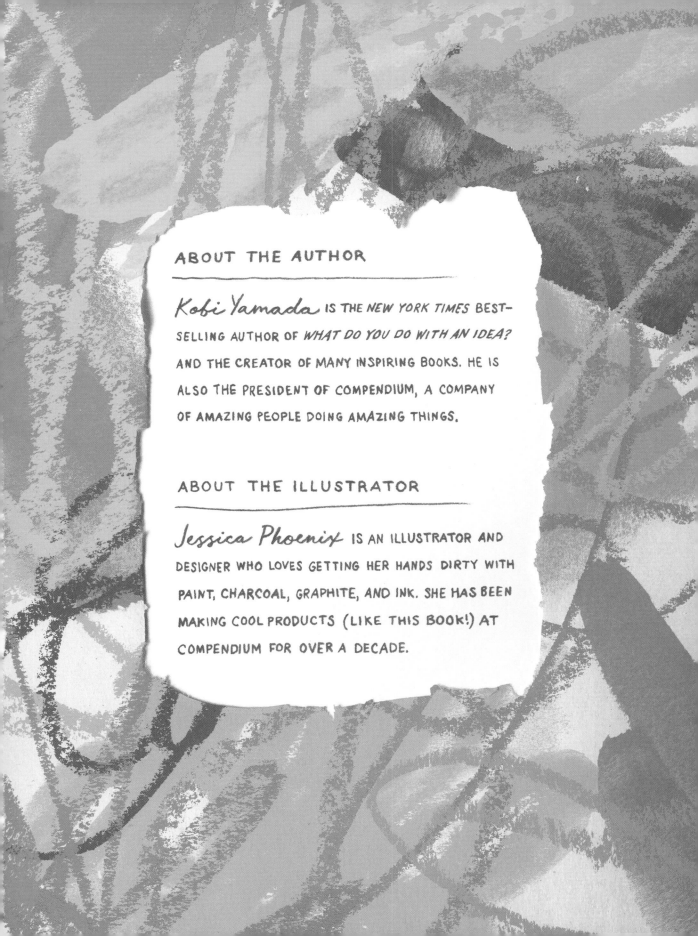

ABOUT THE AUTHOR

Kobi Yamada IS THE *NEW YORK TIMES* BEST-SELLING AUTHOR OF *WHAT DO YOU DO WITH AN IDEA?* AND THE CREATOR OF MANY INSPIRING BOOKS. HE IS ALSO THE PRESIDENT OF COMPENDIUM, A COMPANY OF AMAZING PEOPLE DOING AMAZING THINGS.

ABOUT THE ILLUSTRATOR

Jessica Phoenix IS AN ILLUSTRATOR AND DESIGNER WHO LOVES GETTING HER HANDS DIRTY WITH PAINT, CHARCOAL, GRAPHITE, AND INK. SHE HAS BEEN MAKING COOL PRODUCTS (LIKE THIS BOOK!) AT COMPENDIUM FOR OVER A DECADE.